A drawing of the south front of the former 18th-century coach-house of Hendford Manor. Since 1965 this has housed the Museum of South Somerset, formerly the Yeovil Wyndham Museum. Completely reorganised in 1990-1, to display exhibits in a modern manner, it also possesses an extensive collection of paintings, prints and photographs relating to the area.

YEOVIL
A Pictorial History

Among the earliest of Yeovil's amateur photographers whose work has survived, Henry Stiby, later Mayor and Freeman of the Borough, was himself photographed with his camera at Thorne Coffin church, *c.*1875. A man of many hobbies, he also assembled a large collection of guns demonstrating the development of firing mechanisms, and coin specimens, both now forming part of the museum collection.

YEOVIL
A Pictorial History

Leslie Brooke

with illustrations from the
Museum of South Somerset

Phillimore

1994

Published by
PHILLIMORE & CO. LTD.,
Shopwyke Manor Barn, Chichester, West Sussex

ISBN 0 85033 905 7

Printed and bound in Great Britain by
BIDDLES LTD.
Guildford, Surrey

List of Illustrations

Frontispiece: Henry Stiby with camera, *c.*1875

The Town That Was
1. Porter's Lane, 1924
2. High Street, *c.*1930
3. High Street, *c.*1880
4. Frederick Taylor's construction
5. Frederick Taylor's two-storey building, *c.*1930
6. The Borough, *c.*1930
7. Silver Street, 1960
8. Market Street houses, 1956
9. *George Inn*, Middle Street, 1955
10. *George Inn* demolition, 1962
11. Site of *George Inn*, 1963
12. Approaching the 'Triangle'
13. South Western Terrace, *c.*1880
14. Yeovil bridge, *c.*1880
15. Lower South Street, *c.*1920
16. South Street opposite Penn Hill, *c.*1965
17. Hendford, *c.*1870-80
18. *Three Choughs Hotel*, Hendford, *c.*1900
19. Hendford, site of Homeville flats, *c.*1965
20. Hendford Hill, *c.*1920
21. Lower Hendford Hill, 1965
22. Brunswick Street looking west, *c.*1965
23. No.63 Park Street onwards, 1958
24. Rear of houses, Park Street, 1955
25. *The Rifleman's Arms*, Park Street, *c.*1960
26. Napier House, Park Street, 1956
27. Cottages in Huish, 1955
28. *Royal Standard Inn*, Huish, 1959
29. Farley Gardens, Huish, 1967
30. Princes Street, stereographic pair, *c.*1870-80
31. Building construction, Princes Street
32. Kingston, *c.*1880
33. Cottages, Higher Kingston, 1956
34. Cottages, Higher Kingston, 1955
35. *Nag's Head Inn*, Reckleford, 1962
36. Reckleford Cross, 1965
37. Reckleford, 1960
38. The corner shop, Wyndham Street, 1960
39. *Britannia Inn*, Vicarage Street, 1968
40. Cottages, Vicarage Street, 1958
41. Quidham Place, 1931
42. Vicarage Street, 1960

Civic Government and Public Service
43. Policeman on point duty, *c.*1920
44. Mayor and officials, Ninesprings, 1933
45. Former post office, Middle Street, 1933
46. Mayor buying stamps, new post office, 1932
47. Trades fair opening, 1954
48. Mayoral procession, 1954
49. Borough centenary celebrations, 1954
50. Borough centenary celebrations, 1954
51. Veteran Car Rally, 1954

Getting About
52. Quicksilver Mail, inn sign, 1965
53. Middle Street, *c.*1900
54. South Street, horse omnibus, *c.*1900
55. Corner of High Street and Princes Street, *c.*1900
56. Staff outing, *c.*1890
57. Pickford's horse-drawn furniture van
58. Co-op bread delivery vans, 1939
59. Former Hendford station, 1968
60. Yeovil Town railway station, *c.*1880
61. Bird Brothers' coach outing, 1920
62. Co-op motor vans, 1939
63. Old Station Road, *c.*1965
64. George Rogers' motorised bicycle

Living Quarters
65. Lyde House, 1868
66. Old Sarum House, 1938
67. Swallowcliffe House, 1967
68. No.28 Kingston, 1968
69. Thomas Fooks' house, South Street, *c.*1965
70. Henry Stiby's study
71. Swiss Cottage, Hendford Hill, *c.*1965
72. Hendford Manor lodge
73. Park Road, *c.*1965
74. Rebuilt Kingston toll-house, *c.*1965
75. Hendford Terrace, *c.*1965
76. Vincent Street, *c.*1965
77. Earle Street, *c.*1965
78. Vicarage Street houses, 1958
79. Sparrow Road cottages, 1956
80. Nos.251-3 Preston Road, 1957
81. Jubilee Cottages, Preston Road, 1931

82. Housing scheme opening, 1913
83. Larkhill pre-fabricated houses, 1965

Learning
84. Grammar School scholars, *c*.1750
85. Kingston County School, *c*.1930
86. Reckleford School staff, 1880
87. South Street School, *c*.1880
88. Adult School Band, *c*.1905
89. Wyndham Museum, Kingston, *c*.1965
90. Kingston Museum interior
91. King George Street Museum interior, *c*.1930

Industry
92. Westland woodworkers, 1918
93. Westland woodmill department, 1918
94. Westland propeller department, 1918
95. Westland Widgeon Mark IIIA, 1929
96. Interceptor with Jupiter engine, 1931
97. Leather-dressing yard, Blake & Fox, 1924
98. Unhairing department, Blake & Fox, 1924
99. Wheeling department, Blake & Fox, 1924
100. Glove-cutters, Clothier & Giles, 1955
101. Employees, Eastland Road leather-dressing yard
102. Brewers' offices, Princes Street, 1960
103. Aplin & Barrett's factory, 1898
104. Aplin & Barrett's cheese-making department

Before Supermarkets
105. Honeycombe's grocery shop, *c*.1900
106. Cards' tailors, Hendford, *c*.1900
107. Damon Brothers' shops, Borough, *c*.1900
108. Moffatts' cycle store, High Street
109. Denners' store extension, 1934
110. D. Lawrence, butcher's shop, 1935
111. J. S. Robins' fish and fruit shop
112. Clements' Corner Stores, *c*.1965
113. High Street stores, *c*.1965
114. Percy Winsor's stores, Vicarage Street
115. Boot's chemists, The Borough
116. Rebuilding International Stores
117. Co-operative branch, Orchard Street, 1897
118. Co-operative central store, 1905
119. Hinton Farm Meat Supplies, 1910
120. Entrance to Middle Street, *c*.1890
121. Lower Middle Street, *c*.1965
122. Lower Middle Street, *c*.1965
123. Lower Middle Street, *c*.1965

Spiritual Needs
124. St John the Baptist church, pre-1856
125. Holy Trinity church, 1846
126. Holy Trinity church interior, *c*.1880
127. Christ Church, The Park, *c*.1880
128. Christ Church interior, *c*.1880
129. Unitarian chapel, Vicarage Street, *c*.1965
130. Congregational church, Clarence Street, *c*.1965

131. Methodist meeting-house, Middle Street, *c*.1965
132. Pen Mill Methodist chapel, pre-1914
133. Opening Salvation Army Hall, 1932

Health and Welfare
134. Fiveways hospital, *c*.1880
135. General Hospital opening, 1923
136. Entrance to Yeovil General Hospital
137. Woborn Almshouse, Bond Street
138. Common room of Woborn Almshouse
139. Dorcas House foundation stone laying, 1910
140. Victoria Temperance Hall, *c*.1965

Matters Martial
141. Yeovil Military Band, 1892
142. Yeovil Military Band, pre-1914
143. National Reservists, 1914
144. Recruits, Yeovil Town station, 1914
145. Horses for war service, 1914
146. Nautilus works munitions production
147. V.A.D. officers, Newnam Hall, 1915-8
148. Bomb damage, Rickett's factory, 1940
149. Bomb damage, Rickett's factory, 1940
150. Air-raid shelters, Picketty Row
151. Book recovery, Newnam Hall, 1943
152. Q Section, No.5 Platoon Home Guard, 1944
153. Borough Fire Guard, 1945
154. V.E. Day celebrations, 1945
155. V.E. Day celebrations, 1945
156. V.E. Day celebrations, 1945
157. V.E. Day celebrations, 1945
158. Street party, Orchard Street, 1945

Red-Letter Days
159. Wyndham Fields Queen Victoria's jubilee, 1887
160. Proclamation, Edward VII, 1901
161. Snow in April, 1908
162. George V coronation day, Preston Park, 1911
163. Meet of Hunt in Borough, *c*.1910
164. Labour Sunday procession, 1914
165. Westland Roman pavement, 1927
166. Bath and West Show, Barwick Park, 1932
167. Naming *Yeovil* railway engine, 1945
168. Queen Elizabeth II proclamation, 1952
169. Wellington Street decorations, 1953

Social Occasions
170. Skating on the river Yeo, 1891
171. *Red Lion* outing, 1893
172. Rifle Volunteers' shooting match, 1894
173. Yeovil Thursday Football Club, 1923
174. Marathon race competitors, 1914
175. Yeovil Bowling Club inauguration, 1909
176. Yeovil Cycling Club members, 1931
177. Opening Mudford Road Recreation Ground, 1931
178. Football fans at Manchester, 1949

Acknowledgements

Copyright of all photographs has been vested in the Museum of South Somerset.

Author, front cover illustration, 9, 84; *Bristol Evening Post*, 44, 47, 51; *Bristol Evening Times*, 101; T. J. Cave, 6, 11, 16, 19, 21, 22, 23, 36, 52, 63, 69, 71, 73, 74, 75, 76, 77, 83, 89, 102, 112, 113, 121, 122, 123, 129, 130, 131, 136, 140; H. A. Cooper, 167; Adam Gosney, 13, 54, 60, 126; L. C. Hayward, 67, 68; John Linn, 1; W. H. Rendell, 8, 27, 31, 34, 35, 39, 48, 49, 50, 100, 168; W. S. Rendell, 165; Henry Stiby, frontispiece, 3, 14, 70, 87, 127, 128, 134, 160; Harry Stone, 148, 149; L. Tavender, 7, 10, 28, 33, 37, 38, 42, 59, 79, 80; Brian Tilzey, 169; Harold C. Tilzey, 24, 25, 26, 40, 66, 78, 104, 109, 137, 138, 153; C. J. Trask, 141; Westland Aircraft Co., 95, 96; Witcomb & Son, 41, 81, 82, 110, 116, 133, 139, 143, 166, 173; Yeovil Co-operative Society, 58, 62, 117, 118.

From the Curator, Museum of South Somerset

This book is dedicated to all the people of Yeovil, past, present, and future.

The photographs which make up this volume help both to preserve and illustrate the history of the town. They are a small part of the substantial collection of photographs that have been acquired since Alderman W. R. E. Mitchelmore, Mayor of Yeovil, 1918-21, brought together many examples of antiquities to establish the nucleus of the present Museum of South Somerset.

The discipline of social history is, in academic terms, fairly young and its introduction into museums is a recent phenomenon. Photographs are among the most prolific collections in social history, and museums and historians are extremely selective in their acquisition and use of such a medium.

Photography has now taken on a new role in museums: they rely upon it to provide the 'look of the past' in sites and displays which aim both to interpret and recreate history. The Museum of South Somerset has recently commissioned a photographic record of Yeovil which was carried out during the summer and autumn of 1993. The project will bring visual evidence of Yeovil's development up to date, and is the widest survey of Yeovil commissioned at any one given time. This record of urban expansion will provide a very comprehensive view of Yeovil and will be of great interest to future generations.

If readers of this book consider they have a photograph which may be of interest, or may complement the museum's existing collection, I would be very happy to have a copy made, and record its provenance.

The Museum of South Somerset is located in the old coach house of Hendford Manor, adjacent to the Octagon Theatre, in Yeovil. It was registered with the Museums and Galleries Commission in November 1990, and is administered by the South Somerset District Council.

The illustrations in this book represent just one facet of the museum's collections and the modern displays of local social history will well repay a visit.

MARION BARNES

Introduction

When Thomas Gerard wrote of Yeovil in 1633, he stated: 'I cannot commend the town for the beauty of it', though he did add: 'yet of late some have begun to rebuild'. So perhaps it is not surprising that, though lying on the coach road between London and Exeter, Yeovil received but scant attention pictorially until the advent of photography and, even then, the camera did not record the local scene to any extent until the last quarter of the 19th century.

Indeed, until the early part of the present century, much of Yeovil retained a distinctly rural appearance. At the beginning of the 19th century, the whole parish, excluding Preston, boasted a population of only 2,774—no separate figure being given for the borough. However, rapid expansion followed, and by 1851 the total for the parish was 7,743 and when the century closed the borough's population was 11,704.

Two oil paintings (one of those a doubtful Yeovil scene!), a few pencil sketches, watercolours, and lithographs pre-date photography and, even then, one can understand the reluctance of early itinerant 'photographic artists' to produce more than a few saleable views from a small and mostly unattractive town, since this necessitated coating 'wet plates' with light-sensitive emulsion, loading them into dark slides, and then into a bulky plate camera, make time exposures, then develop negatives in a portable darkroom, before producing prints by means of daylight exposure in frames.

Towards the end of the century, however, a notable resident, Henry Stiby, one-time Mayor, Sunday school superintendent and firearms collector, had added photography to his many hobbies, and the Museum of South Somerset possesses a collection of some of his half-plate glass negatives consisting largely of neighbourhood churches, but also including Yeovil street scenes, with many buildings long since disappeared.

The museum collection, following Stiby's day, has been expanded by works of local artists and photographers, though it is a matter for regret that negatives of several professional photographers, who flourished before the Second World War, were destroyed. But a debt of gratitude is due to all those recorders of the local scene who have so generously donated their works. Among the many donors, names of those who are known have been accredited, though there are many, particularly of the early period, who remain unknown—all too frequently gifts of prints contain no indication either as to the originator, subject, or date. It is only by local knowledge and comparison with others, that, in many instances, tentative allocation of such information can be assigned.

There have been several publications of Yeovil photographic scenes, including many from the museum collection, though none are so extensive as this present volume. As far as possible, repetition of those has been avoided and preference given to hitherto unpublished material, scenes from a different viewpoint, or of different date.

The task of examining the whole of the musuem collection of local illustrations has been rendered much less arduous through the invaluable assistance of the author's wife and by members of the Friends of the museum. Particular thanks are due to the curator, Miss Marion Barnes and her assistant, Mr. T. Stok, to Mr. M. D. Shorter, A.R.P.S. for making copies of originals, and to the publishers for the opportunity of rendering this book possible.

The Town That Was

The earliest known map of Yeovil, being of the comparatively recent date of 1806, shows that the town had hardly expanded at all beyond the confines of the tiny medieval borough. Recollections of an old Yeovilian in 1892, relating to a period some 30 years after the map was drawn, speak of the swampy nature of lower Middle Street where 'a rough stone wall enclosed fields where only stunted withy trees grew', aggravated by two streams, little more than open sewers, which converged from different directions to pass under a low bridge where now the pedestrian precinct passes in front of the Liberal Club. The effluent was eventually absorbed into the Dodham Brook.

Improvement, slow at first, gathered momentum with a boom in the leather and glove industry, together with civic awareness of the need to provide an effective body to deal with the town's sanitary and living standards generally. Coupled with this was an increase in middle-class wealth, together with a blossoming in the number of traders attracted here, to cater more effectively for local demand, than could readily be met through Yeovil's weekly market, prosperous though that had been since medieval times. Indeed, the necessity for change from a still largely medieval-orientated system had been long overdue, and the town began to adapt to modern requirements. By the turn of the century, large new residential areas were already being established, a continuing trend which only paused for two world wars.

By the 1950s it was quite evident that the ancient narrow streets and roads were quite inadequate to deal with the ever-increasing flow of mechanised traffic. Town-centre accidents led firstly to the introduction of one-way systems, and then, where possible, to the total closure of parts of streets for pedestrian use only.

Of course, there were protests as perfectly good terraces of houses were demolished to make way for car parks, or coach and bus stations, while planners were accused of short-sightedness when they laid out schemes for dual-carriageway ring roads.

Among the many thriving towns which were not compelled to rebuild extensively, as the result of war damage, Yeovil must certainly qualify as being among the foremost to exhibit a greatly altered face. Like most with a reputation as a local shopping centre, it has suffered the loss of the majority of its once well-known individual storekeepers, who found it impossible to compete on equal terms with multi-national firms; though there are still some who can claim a direct descent from names of traders whose advertisements are to be found in directories and almanacs spanning a 40-year period from 1880. Although a large number of public houses in the town centre have fallen to the actions of the demolition contractor, none have been more regretted then the removal in 1962 of the half-timbered *George Hotel* from Middle Street, which had been owned from 1478 to 1920 by the trustees of Woborn's almshouses. Tradition asserts that it was to this establishment, in 1647, that a traveller from London brought with him the plague which resulted in the deaths of hundreds of townsfolk.

In the section which follows, once-familiar street scenes date largely from the 1950s and '60s, though interspersed are views which date from about 1870 onwards.

. Porter's Lane, a sketch by John Linn, 1924, showing a view towards High
treet from the narrow lane which preceded Westminster Street. Forming part
f Huish, it was popularly called 'Porter's' from William Porter, whose
ookseller's and printing establishment stood at its entrance in the early 19th
entury.

. High Street, c.1930. Increase in traffic had yet to render a pedestrian
rossing necessary at the spot where the photographer stood to record this
cene. However, presaging the future, a motor-cycle with sidecar stands
utside Moffatt's cycle shop (now Southern Electricity) where signs show that
hell and Pratt's Motor Spirit was on sale to motorists.

3.   Another view of High Street, taken *c*.1880 by Henry Stiby, which defines the carriageway by means of stone guttering, the spaces on either side being occupied by stall-holders on market days. The town hall, burnt down in 1935, shows its original clock tower, which was taken down in 1887 and not replaced until 1913.

Following the decision in the early 1920s to lay out
street on the site of the former Borough House and to
construct new municipal offices on the west side, Messrs.
Frederick Taylor took the opportunity to start work on a
department store on the north-east corner site.

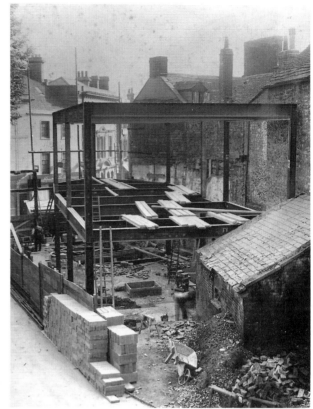

Erected on the site of old buildings adjoining the
garden approach to The Borough House, Frederick
Taylor's store was at first a two-storey building, and the
earliest in the town to employ the use of reconstituted
stone. Expanding business led to a third floor being added
before the Second World War, when the store became
Plummer Roddis Ltd.

6. The town's ancient market place, known from early times as The Borough though actually forming part of the High Street, is now devoid of market stalls. Access for traffic behind the war memorial is no longer possible, and for many years, cars have not been allowed to travel in a westerly direction as did the two shown in this photograph, which dates from the 1930s

7. Occupied by the Corn Market in medieval times, this portion of Silver Street, as it was in 1960, has been transformed on its eastern side by a side entrance to Marks & Spencer's stores, whilst the entrance to the former Vicarage Street has become a ramp to the Quedam shopping centre, with toilets adjoining.

8. These Market Street dwellings, photographed on 8 January 1956, have since entirely disappeared, together with the rest of the homes which lined both sides of the street. For the first 30 years of the 19th century this was the original Reckleford and lay outside the borough boundary.

9. The *George Hotel*, Middle Street, was built for a wealthy Yeovil merchant as a private dwelling house; it became the *Three Cups Inn* in 1642. Renamed the *George* early in the 19th century— perhaps a transfer from an earlier *George* in The Borough—and dignified as an 'hotel', it had never been more than a small inn, not even for coaching!

10.   Demolished for road-widening in 1962, in spite of protests, a leaded window from the *George Inn* is now displayed in the Museum of South Somerset, other windows being used in a Dorset cottage. Hand-made tiles replaced a slate roof at Coat's Little Manor, near Martock, and beams and brackets were incorporated in a house at Ash.

11.   When the *George* had been removed, ostensibly to widen the road, the owners of the store which replaced it refused for a time to allow the space gained to be so used. This picture shows the site of the inn's projection by inserted kerb-stones. When, eventually, the space was incorporated, only a short while elapsed before the street was pedestrianised.

12. Although this postcard is entitled the 'Triangle', this scene shows the approach to it, where once there was a triangle of land with cottages, separated from the buildings between Middle and South Streets by Turnstile Lane. This was the medieval Vennell's Cross separating the ancient borough from Fore Street, now lower Middle Street.

13. Photographed *c.*1880, South Western Terrace is now in Old Station Road. It was built after the opening of Yeovil Town railway station in 1861. Gateway Stores now occupies the site of Bradford & Sons' coal yard, while the wall of the *Temperance Hotel,* on the left hand side of the picture, shows that it possessed 'well-aired beds'.

14. Leland described this bridge 'of three great Arches of Stone' over the river Yeo in 1540. Henry Stiby's photograph of *c*.1880 shows those arches which, suffered damage by U.S.A. military vehicles during the Second World War, necessitating the rebuilding and widening the visible side. The toll-house is in Dorset, the river here acting as the county boundary.

15.   Lower South Street, *c*.1920. The large light-coloured building on the right was a box-making works, a site later occupied by Somerset & Dorset Box Co. Ltd (A. Stevens & Co. Ltd.). The buildings beyond, including Pashen's, or Patience, Court, were replaced by the Gaumont Cinema, which extended the site of the former Palace Theatre.

16.   South Street opposite Penn Hill, *c*.1965. The lodge on the left stood at the driveway entrance to Penn House and the private grounds of Peter Daniell in the early 19th century. The buildings opposite were extensions to Messrs. Hill, Sawtell Ltd. in High Street, the recessed building now being a pharmacy.

17. Hendford, from one half of a stereographic pair, dating from possibly 1870-80. The building on the right was Stuckey's (later Westminster) Bank. Opposite, all that is now Denners was Edwards & Dean, drapers, then Frederick Dobell, watchmaker and jeweller, Richard Bradshaw, draper, Exell & Son, tailors, and the barber's pole belonged to W. C. Hann, fishmonger and hair cutter!

18. Hendford: A horse bus with passengers from town stations arrives at the *Three Choughs Hotel*. The driver is perched on a typical basketwork luggage container such as that used by commercial travellers and theatrical performers. Other trunks are lashed to the top of the coach. Note the hand-cart on the left loaded with mattresses.

19. Hendford, *c*.1965, now the site of Homeville flats. Part of the former St John's parish vicarage is on the right, while old properties in the centre of the picture include the one-time *London Inn*.

20. Hendford Hill, *c*.1920. This road was constructed and improved by Yeovil and District Turnpike Trust in the 1760s, when a toll-house stood on the left, with gates across the foreground, where there is now a large and busy roundabout. Sheep being driven down the hill were once a familiar sight on market days.

21.   Almost devoid of traffic, this 1965 view of the lower part of Hendford Hill is in stark contrast to the scene today. Aldon Terrace, on the right with the just visible *Railway Hotel* beyond, came into being after the opening nearby of Yeovil's first railway station in 1853. Like the station, all the other buildings shown here have since disappeared.

22.   Brunswick Street, *c.*1965. The steps on the right, leading between a modern and older buildings, followed the route of the original Addlewell Lane. Subsequently this became known as Chant's Path, which was finally extinguished with the removal of most of the older properties shown here.

23. No.63 Park Street and onwards, 1958. This street was laid out on Peter Daniell's Penn Hill grounds, and was first shown on E. Watts' map of Yeovil of 1831. Town Commissioners' minutes for 1834 show preparations for 'completing the new road' and the allocation of £140 for that purpose, 'to be repaid by the owners of property in the street'.

24. A rear view of the houses on the south side of Park Street, showing how they were stacked on the steep hillside. Houses in the street were mainly occupied by workers in the glove industry.

25.   Nos.28, 30 and 32 Park Street, including the *Rifleman's Arms*, a beer-house held by Walter Pardy, who was also agent for 'Foster's parcel deliveries'. The house on the right was that of decorators Tucker & Hawkins. Most of the original street properties were demolished *c*.1960.

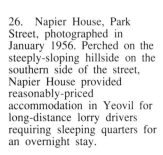

26.   Napier House, Park Street, photographed in January 1956. Perched on the steeply-sloping hillside on the southern side of the street, Napier House provided reasonably-priced accommodation in Yeovil for long-distance lorry drivers requiring sleeping quarters for an overnight stay.

27.   Cottages in Huish, approaching Wellington Street and opposite Yeovil's first National School, when demolition was taking place in 1955, prior to redevelopment and the building of Wellington Flats. The former *Crown Inn* is on the left.

28. Demolition   of the *Royal Standard Inn* in Wellington Street in progress in September 1959. When first opened here its address was given as Huish, and the name of the inn was perpetuated shortly afterwards by a new fully-licensed public house in Larkhill.

29.   Farley Gardens, which were said to have been the first development in Huish. This photograph, dated February 1967, was taken shortly before demolition took place. The Farley family have had local connections since the 16th century.

30.   Amongst the earliest photographic records of Yeovil are a few faded stereographic pairs which have survived. Although undated, it is estimated that this example of Princes Street is one of a series produced between 1870 and 1880, when the novelty of a 3D effect was produced by looking through a special viewer.

31. Showing curved steelwork by Messrs. F. W. Sibley & Co. Ltd., this building being erected by Messrs. D. Singleton & Son was built for Burtol Cleaners on the corner of Park Road and Princes Street. Shortly afterwards it was acquired by Messrs. Griffith & Palmer, house agents, and it is now occupied by estate agent, Tony Collard.

32. One of a stereographic pair, dating from *c.*1870-80, showing Kingston. The building on the left, with steps on either side leading to a central door, became the *Kingston Hotel.* The large house next to it, with iron posts and chains in front, was the residence of Dr. E. C. Garland, medical officer of health. All the buildings shown in this scene have long since disappeared.

33.   A row of six cottages in Higher Kingston, demolished in 1969 to clear a site for the building of hospital staff accommodation. The building on the right, Pitney House, was the residence of former solicitor, Mr. T. Moore. It was taken down when the new Yeovil District Hospital was built. The photograph dates from 1956.

34.   Cottages at the corner of Higher Kingston and Roping Road, photographed in 1955. Built of local stone, they projected into the roadway, pre-dating the cottages shown in illustration 33. The cottages were demolished in 1969 and the site was used to widen the road and to erect a block of flats to accommodate hospital nurses.

35. A *Nag's Head* is mentioned in Yeovil leases of 1727 and 1751, when R. Cuff was licensee. However, it is unlikely that they referred to this Reckleford public house, which was demolished in 1963 for construction of Stage I of Yeovil's inner relief road.

36. The junction of Market Street with Reckleford still retained the name Reckleford Cross when this photograph was taken showing demolition of the corner buildings in progress in 1965. A wayside cross once stood in the middle of the road here, shown on E. Watts' 1806 map of Yeovil. Earlier in the century the Misses Chaffey kept Reckleford Cross School just inside Market Street.

37. Reckleford, 4 December 1960. The terrace, on the left, adjoining the *Glovers' Arms*, was removed for road widening and for the construction of the ambulance and fire stations, which were opened in 1962. Salisbury Terrace, further along, disappeared a little later, together with the cottages on the right, which were built by William Dampier, *c*.1850, to house his glove workers.

38. The corner shop and adjoining house were removed from the corner of Wyndham Street and Reckleford not long after this photograph was taken on 4 December 1960.

39. The licence of an earlier *Britannia Inn* in Park Street had been transferred to the Elizabethan building in Vicarage Street early in the 1860s. A fire in 1880 caused some rebuilding, but it was not until 1969 that the building was taken down and the stonework reused to construct a house at Ash near Martock.

40. Many old houses in Vicarage Street, which once housed workers in the gloving industry, had fallen victim to the demolition contractor, to provide parking spaces, long before the street was almost totally wiped out with the development of the Quedam Centre. Already boarded up in 1958, these cottages stood opposite the Methodist church.

41. The narrow entrance to Quidham Place in the former Vicarage Street, photographed in 1931. The area was cleared in 1968, but its name retained a corrupted form of the Latin word *quedam*, a medieval attribution to a street of unknown name before St John's vicarage was sited there in the 14th century.

42. A 1960 view of the western portion of Vicarage Street. Vicarage Street Hall, on the left, was a short distance around the corner from Frederick Place. The hall, built as a Sunday School for St John's in 1818, was used for some time as British Schools and subsequently by Christian Brethren.

Civic Government and Public Service

In 1954 celebrations were held to mark the centenary of the transition of local government from Portreeve and Burgesses, coupled with Improvement and Special Commissioners, to a Mayor, Aldermen, and Councillors representing the 'Municipal Borough'. Until then, the ancient borough had been confined to an area of some 15 acres (six hectares) in the centre of which was the open space serving as a market square and which, today, is referred to as The Borough, though officially it is only a part of High Street.

This market square was once occupied by a so-called 'market-house'—a covered 70 ft. by 20ft. area consisting of a stone-tiled roof supported on 20 stone pillars—in the centre of which were the remains of an ancient market cross and the town stocks. These filled the space now more or less taken up by reserved car parking for disabled persons. On the other side of the square, separated by a throughway for carts and carriages, were covered butchers' shambles standing in front of the Portreeve's court chamber and market toll-house, which occupied the site of the present sports equipment shop.

The portreeve, chosen from a body of burgesses since the 12th century and approved of by the lord of the manor, governed well enough as magistrate in the court leet, but by the early 19th century, his limited powers caused dissatisfaction and prominent townsmen obtained an act in 1830 appointing Improvement Commissioners to set about amending streets and overseeing a police force. A further act in 1846 appointed Special Commissioners to set about improving market conditions. The jurisdiction of the once-powerful lord of the manor, together with those of the bodies referred to above, were all incorporated into the municipal borough which came into being on 3 July 1954.

The police force of 1830 consisted of two constables, augmented by two watchmen and a day-time beadle; it was not until 1845 that a full-time Police and Watch Superintendent was appointed. When the local force came under the County Constabulary in 1858, it comprised a sergeant and four constables, housed in a police station with three cells, in Union Street. Known as the Town House, it also accommodated the Town Surveyor, and today is occupied by Yeovil Town Council.

Once the private grounds of Aldon House, Ninesprings, Yeovil's prime beauty spot of 40 acres of natural woodland, now looked after by South Somerset District Council, was first leased as one of its parks by Yeovil Town Council in 1932, when over 2,000 visitors were recorded during the Easter weekend alone. Teas were obtainable during the summer months from a former thatched cottage, standing above one of the lakes.

Owing to the lapse of the lease, due to change of ownership, and the period of neglect which followed, the cottage became derelict and fell into ruin. It was eventually acquired by the council. In 1974 a Ninesprings Conservation Trust was set up which carried out a major restoration programme. A marshy area was converted into a lake which is now the habitat of a variety of wildfowl.

43. A familiar sight, before traffic proliferated to today's level, was a policeman on point duty at busy junctions in the town. Here, a constable with white gloves stands where now a mini-roundabout serves the purpose at the junction of South Street and Hendford. The presence of the boy is not accounted for—was he lost? The date is *c.*1920.

44. The Mayor, members of the Town Council and officials with their wives, at Ninesprings on Thursday, 4 May 1933, at the invitation of the owner, Major H. C. C. Batten. Until the previous year, when it was leased to the corporation, visits to the beauty spot were only possible by ticket obtainable from the owner through the town clerk's office.

45. This Middle Street building, erected in 1902, replaced Princes Street premises where Yeovil's post office had been located since moving from Silver Street in 1876. In turn, this was supplanted by a new building in King George Street, opened in 1932, and these vacated premises were taken over by Marks & Spencer in 1933, where they remained until 1972.

46. The Mayor, Alderman W. E. Tucker, buying the first postage stamps to be issued from the new post office in King George Street in 1932. The post office occupied the whole of the block on the eastern side of the street until 1965, when Huish premises came into operation and Barclay's Bank took over a substantial portion of the building.

47. As part of the Yeovil Corporation centenary celebrations, 1954, a trades fair was held in the grounds of Hendford Manor. This photograph shows the opening ceremony being performed by Marshal of the Royal Air Force, Sir John Slessor, G.C.B, D.S.O., M.C.

48. A civic service was held in St John's church on 3 July 1954 to mark the Corporation's centenary, attended by civic dignitaries from other boroughs. Here, led by the mace-bearer (Mr. Eveleigh) are the Mayor, Alderman W. B. Hickman, accompanied by Town Clerk, Mr. T. S. Jewels, and followed by His Honour Judge Armstrong and the Mayor of Weston-super-Mare.

49. Yeovil Corporation centenary celebrations, 1954. Among those attending the civic service were contingents from the Royal Naval Association, the British Legion, and the Army Cadet Force, seen here proceeding through Princes Street.

50. Yeovil Corporation centenary celebrations, 1954. The procession which marched through the streets of the town, is seen here preceded by the band of H.M. Royal Marines, Portsmouth, in lower Middle Street.

51. Yeovil Corporation centenary celebrations, 1954. Among the many events was a veteran car rally, which assembled in the grounds of Hendford Manor, before touring through the main streets. The Mayor and Mayoress, Alderman and Mrs. W. B. Hickman, are here seen with V.V.C. No. 14, a 1905 Coupelle.

Getting About

Narrow streets, where buildings projected at odd angles beyond neighbouring properties, were a legacy from the medieval plan of the small country town that Yeovil still was at the beginning of the 19th century.

As the century progressed, traffic increased proportionately to the growth of trade and industry. A contributing factor, in the second half of the century, was the opening of the railway line which brought travellers and goods from afar, who then used local transport for distribution.

Throughout the century, however, the horse continued to be the principal means of transport, whether by pony and trap, carriage and pair, or by wagonette, and there were several local coach-makers providing employment to local craftsmen.

Yeovil on market days was crowded, as people from neighbouring villages abandoned vehicles in search of 'market ordinaries' which were a common feature of most of the town's hostelries; market traders, too, added to the congestion as their stalls occupied the roadway, and horse-dealers paraded mounts for the benefit of potential buyers.

The 20th century brought fresh problems as the motor car gradually became commonplace. Traffic control at busy intersections was first provided by point-duty policemen, but as volume increased controlled crossings and one-way systems were instituted, as well as the construction of roundabouts. Start, too, was made on the building of a ring-road.

Public transport provided a rapid means of reaching the town from south Somerset and neighbouring Dorset villages, while 'town services' afforded shoppers from the newly-built housing estates on the edge of Yeovil a less tiring and more rapid expedition to the centre, for the expenditure of only a penny or two.

52. This former inn sign of the *Quicksilver Mail* at the top of Hendford Hill shows the mailcoach of that name in the 1830s, which was the fastest between Exeter and London, and which is said to have used this inn as one of its staging-posts where horses were changed.

53. Middle Street, anciently Pit Lane, despite having been widened in places by Town Commissioners in the 1830s, still retained much of its medieval character at the turn of the century when this postcard was produced. In places it had been only 11ft. 9ins. wide, and, as apparent here opposite the *George Hotel*, liable to congestion, even prior to the motor car.

54. South Street, *c.*1900. Standing outside the *Greyhound Hotel* is the horse-omnibus which plied between the town centre and the railway stations. Next door was the *Cow Inn*, while on the opposite side of the street is the *Globe and Crown*, only recently converted (1993) to the Globetrotters Restaurant.

55. Vehicular traffic at the junction of High Street, Hendford, and Princes Street, also about the turn of the century. The corner building had been built for the Capital and Counties Bank, and opened in 1897. It was subsequently occupied by the National Provincial Bank, and is now the Yeovil offices of the Bristol and West Building Society.

56. *(Left)* Before motor-coaches, annual staff outings tended to be leisurely affairs restricted to beauty spots within a reasonable radius. The two dozen or so staff of Messrs. Whitby Brothers' glove manufactory are seen here at Batcombe Down, *c.*1890, an event which was typical of expeditions organised by other of the town's larger gloving firms.

57. *(Below left)* Pickfords' horse-drawn furniture removal vans, direct descendants of the old-time carriers, were still commonplace well into the present century. Other local carriers, such as Chaplin & Co. in Hendford, and some local stores, also provided a similar service, though railway containers were frequently employed for removals involving long distances.

58. *(Below)* Freshly-baked bread delivered to customers' doors was a service provided by Yeovil and District Co-operative Society Ltd., similar to that found in the larger towns of the county. Yeovil's horse-drawn vans served both town and adjacent villages up to and including the Second World War.

59.   Closed under the 'Beeching Axe' in May 1968, this view of part of the Yeovil to Taunton railway line includes, just beyond the 'Whistle' notice, the original Hendford station—a terminus when it was opened in October 1853. After demolition, the local stone used in its construction was employed in repair work on St John's parish church in the 1980s.

60.   Professional photographer Adam Gosney recorded this view of the joint Yeovil Town railway station c.1880. Shared by the London & South Western and the Bristol & Exeter (G.W.R.) railway companies, each with their own stationmaster, it opened on 1 June 1861 and was closed 1 March 1967. Demolished a little later, the site is now a car park.

61.   During the 1920s, the motor-vehicle became a popular means of transport for day-excursions and annual outings during the summer months. This coach, owned by Bird Brothers, Yeovil, was photographed in 1920 with such a party—it bears a notice showing its maximum speed to have been 12 m.p.h.!

62.   In their 1889-1939 jubilee souvenir brochure, Yeovil & District Co-operative Society proudly displayed their fleet of 21 motor-vans on part of the former fairground at the rear of Huish Primary School, all now part of the Tesco complex.

63.   Standing on the corner of Middle Street and South Western Terrace, the former *Fernleigh Temperance Hotel (left)* was offices for Southern National, Royal Blue and Associated Motorways when this scene was photographed *c.*1965. Buses serving local villages line up in Station Road before a supermarket was built on that side of the street, while the station forecourt served as a coach station.

64.   George Rogers, a local builder (1886-1975), is pictured here in an early attempt to lessen the physical effort needed to propel a bicycle up Yeovil's hilly streets by fitting a low-powered engine to the frame. It was soon superseded by the less cumbersome moped

Living Quarters

The report by Dr. T. W. Rammell, an inspector for the General Board of Health, of an inquiry held in 1852 into sanitary conditions in the parish of Yeovil, revealed an enormous disparity in living conditions between the wealthier inhabitants and the lowest paid. Nothing could be more deplorable than the aspect of many dwellings of the latter, which the report described as 'haunts of disease'. Examples of such were cited as being Pashen's Court in South Street, Dean's Court in Middle Street, Jennings' Court in Vicarage Street and Paradise Row, Huish.

Despite its name, conditions in Paradise were anything but salubrious, for there were only two privies for all the inhabitants living in the 18 or 20 houses there. The eight houses comprising Dean's Court were even worse off, for the single privy there was so close to a well that the latter acted as a drain to it, and the water it contained was so polluted as to be completely unusable.

Cottages occupied by 'the lowest and poorest classes' were stated to be let at 1s. 6d. a week, the landlord paying rates and taxes, while many more were let at '2s. 6d. weekly, or £6 10s a year'. A leading tradesman gave evidence that 'when trade is good, as it is now, there is a great deal of overcrowding; but when it is depressed, families crowd very much together to save house rent'. However, he went on to say that there was an increasing disposition among working classes to attend to neatness and comfort in their dwellings.

At the other end of the scale, prosperous members of professions and businesses had already erected stylish dwellings, foremost among them being the early 18th-century Church House, in Church Street, which was built for the Batten family of bankers and solicitors and remains largely intact. On the other hand, the imposing Old Sarum House in Princes Street, of about the same period (illustration 78) was sadly mutilated, though now restored to something of its former dignity. These gentlemen's houses were followed a little later by others, principally in Kingston and Hendford.

Following Dr. Rammell's report and the creation of the municipal borough, much was done to remove slum-like areas, and many terraced streets came into being within the now greatly expanded town boundary.

Into the new century, the Housing and Town Planning Act of 1909 saw plans for development on former farmland. The scheme, started in January 1912, was for Yeovil's first municipal estate at Eastland, the initial stage being completed, as Newtown, a little more than a year later, when the President of the Local Government Board (the equivalent of todays Secretary of State for the Environment), the Rt. Hon. John Burns, performed the opening ceremony. In introducing the Act in 1909, he had stressed that due consideration should be given to amenities in planning new towns. The town council, in following these guidelines, claimed it had provided more efficient housing for the cost expended than any other municipal body, and by 1918 the corporation was recognised as a 'pioneer housing authority'.

Council estates continued to be developed between the wars, and some 1,600 homes were erected, a policy which continued after the end of hostilities in 1945, and some 700 houses were added in the next ten years, as well the 150 pre-fabricated bungalows at Larkhill (illustration 83).

65. An enquiry was received in 1989 by Yeovil public library from an American correspondent, as to the whereabouts of the house in this photograph, which was stated to be Lyde House, Yoevil [sic], residence of the Knott family in 1868. Despite its attractive appearance, it has not been possible to give a positive identification. It is not *Great Lyde* (Inn).

66. Old Sarum House, Princes Street, 1938. Built *c*.1730 by Samuel Dampier the elder, a wealthy clothier, it was inherited by his daughter, Susannah, who married John Ryall, a Yeovil glove manufacturer. Their daughter married George Mayo, a prosperous yeoman farmer, and their son, John Ryall Mayo, who inherited the house in 1818, became Yeovil's first mayor in 1854.

67. At a time of growing prosperity for Yeovil businessmen, the early years of the 19th century, Swallowcliffe House, Kingston, was built (probably for glover George Mayo) by Charles Vining, master mason and builder, c.1810-15. It now houses government offices and is less visible than in this picture, owing to an increased growth of shrubbery.

68. The Moore family residence from at least 1842, no.28 Kingston became the rural district council offices, when meeting places and offices of the council were brought under one roof for the first time in 1928; a purpose-built council chamber was added in 1933. The premises were demolished in January 1969 for road-widening and the construction of Yeovil District Hospital.

69.   The house in the centre of this view down South Street, of late 18th-century date, was the home of Thomas Fooks, an early 19th-century glove manufacturer. He was one of the original Town Commissioners appointed in 1830, and was elected to the Town Council when Yeovil became incorporated in 1854. The house was demolished soon after being photographed, *c*.1965.

70.   Interior views of Yeovil residences in the 19th century are extremely rare—this one is especially interesting since it shows the study of Henry Stiby when he lived at 5 The Park. It includes some of his extensive collection of firearms. Among the early members of Yeovil Volunteer Rifle Corps, he gained the reputation of being an excellent marksman.

71. Standing close to the entrance of Lovers' Lane on Hendford Hill, this building, now destroyed, was called The Lodge in a directory of 1907, while later directories in the 1930s name it Bragg Church Lodge. However, its popular name was Swiss Cottage and it is shown in the Tithe Apportionment of 1846 to have been the property of Frederick Greenham.

72. Hendford Manor Lodge, standing in the grounds of the manor house, had been largely obscured from the road by trees and shrubs, many passers-by being unaware of its presence. Prior to its demolition in the 1970s it was occupied by the Christian Science Society.

73. Park Road, leading from Sidney Gardens to Princes Street, with the 'Armoury' (now a public house) on the right. The dwellings here were of good quality and occupied by 'gentry' and tradesmen when built. Park Way emerged into Park Road at the extreme edge on the left. This row of houses was demolished when Queensway was laid out in 1973.

74. Following the abolition of Yeovil Turnpike Trust in 1875, and the removal of the Kingston gates across the road at the five crossways, the toll-house was taken down, stone by stone, and rebuilt a hundred yards or so nearer the town. It was finally demolished in 1969 for road-widening and the site was cleared for the erection of Yeovil District Hospital.

75.   This not unattractive row of houses, known as Hendford Terrace, lay beyond the grounds of Hendford Manor House, and was separated from them by Chant's Path—the original Addlewell Lane—at the beginning of the 19th century. Pulled down for road-widening, the spot today is a grassy bank on the corner of Brunswick Street.

76.   Only a couple of minutes' walk from the town centre, the former Vincent Street, photographed c.1965, is now an underway entrance to the service area below the Quedam shopping precinct. The car on the right is emerging from the former Earle Street, also almost entirely residential.

77.   Earle Street, with the 'Vincent and Earle Street Stores' on the left—now part of Central Road. These houses were all swept away, those on the left providing an area for a coach station for a while. Subsequent redevelopment re-aligned the roadway and the right-hand side is now covered by the multi-storey car park.

78.   Vicarage Street houses in 1958, opposite its junction with Vincent Street. This was another residential area, once largely occupied by workers in the leather and gloving industry. It was one of the least salubrious parts of the town early in the 19th century, despite its having contained the vicarage of St John's church for over 500 years.

79. Photographed in 1956, these stone-built cottages, looking west, in Sparrow Road, were typical of many such buildings lying on what had been the edge of the town, with relatively small windows and tiny front gardens. Constructed with local ('Yeovil') sandstone, they were affected by heat from fires which caused rapid deterioration to chimneys. The brick replacement is clearly evident here.

80. Nos.251-3 Preston Road. In a provisional list of buildings of architectural or historic interest, compiled in 1948, these cottages were stated to be worthy of Grade II grouping. No.251 was 19th-century or of much restored earlier origin, while no.253 had a 17th-century two-storey splayed bay with stone-mullioned windows above. Photographed in 1957, all have since disappeared.

81. Known as Jubilee Cottages and similar in character to those in the preceding illustration, they faced the 'Jubilee Tree' in Preston Road, which was planted in 1887 to mark Queen Victoria's golden jubilee. Photographed in 1931, they only survived another seven years.

82. In January 1912, work commenced on building Yeovil's first 50 council houses on 200 acres added to the borough in 1903. The importance of this pioneer development was recognised by the housing ministry of the day, the Rt. Hon. John Burns, M.P., performing the opening ceremony in February 1913, seen here with Mayor Joseph Boll and mace-bearer, H. Jesty.

83. Pre-fabricated houses, Larkhill, 1965. Urgent need to provide homes at the end of the Second World War led to keen competition among erectors. Workers on the Larkhill estate in October 1946 created a record, completing such a building, with all services, in 40 minutes 27 seconds. Some 150 'pre-fabs' were completed here in the space of six weeks.

Learning

The existence of a choir school in the parish church in the 15th and 16th centuries can be assumed from wills and churchwardens' accounts. A Yeovil tailor's will, dated 1401, allowed a penny 'to each boy scholar who is present at my exsequies', while another will, of 1406, bequeathed fourpence to 'each boy coming and remaining in a surplice at my obsequies and singing in a proper manner'. In the 16th century, John Stockwell, who seems to have been parish clerk, choirmaster and organist, also appears to have been responsible for teaching the choirboys; an entry in the accounts of 1551 reads, 'to the same John [Stockwell], pay to the Master of the Children for sartin sonngs', 5s. 4d.

Yeovil's first grammar and Latin school for boys was established in what had been a chantry chapel in St John's churchyard. Although purchased in 1549, it was not until 1573 that £12 13s. 4d. was spent on its conversion. In 1707 a charity school was added in the same building, but this was closed in 1884 owing to dwindling attendances.

A school, opened by John Aldridge in Clarence Street in 1845, was soon transferred to a large house in Kingston, to become Kingston School, later extended and renamed Yeovil County School. The school eventually moved to new buildings in Mudford Road, and it was ultimately absorbed in today's Yeovil College.

Among the most successful 'schools for young ladies' was Girton House School, started in the 1880s by Mrs. Nosworthy in Hendford, but relocated in Preston Road, overlooking Sidney Gardens. It was subsequently taken over by Miss Cobb's Grove Avenue School, and later became Yeovil Girls' High School.

Miss Martha Softley opened a school in 1851 in Mudford Road, near the five cross-ways. Following other moves, she was joined by Mrs. M. A. Bennet as co-principal in premises in The Park. As today's Park School, it occupies premises erected in 1976, together with the Regency house in Kingston which had been the Vinings' family home.

The first National School, opened in Huish in 1846, for the education of boys and girls of poor parents 'in the principles of the Church of England', was followed by South Street Schools in 1860.

The 1870 Elementary Education Act resulted in the provision of Yeovil's first 'Board School', in Reckleford, in 1874. Others followed as the century moved towards its close, to meet the needs of an ever-growing population.

In addition to the above, mention should be made of dame schools which were common in the 19th century, providing basic education to young children for a few pence. In April 1871 Yeovil School Board recorded the existence of 11 dame schools, but considered them 'inefficient by reason of incompetency of the teachers and defective accommodation of the premises' —only two 'private venture' schools were said to have been at all efficient.

In addition to the schools, there was a Mechanics Institute which enjoyed a brief existence in Church Street in the 1840s, followed by a Mutual Improvement Society in 1847 which survived until 1880. Further education was also available by the end of the century through evening and adult classes, while a 'Government Art and Science School' in Victoria Hall in 1903 eventually became Yeovil Technical College and School of Art.

84. Yeovil Grammar School scholars going to church, *c*.1750. This detail from an oil painting of St John's parish church shows the medieval chantry chapel, converted into a grammar school in 1573. Taken down and re-erected on a nearby site, it is still known as 'The Chantry', though it has long since ceased to be used as a school.

85. Yeovil County School, on the right, formerly Kingston School founded by John Aldridge, 1845, came under county control in 1905 as provided for by the 1902 Education Act. Moved to buildings in Mudford Road in 1938, it became part of Yeovil College in 1974. This building remained as a Technical School and School of Art, until Yeovil Technical College opened in 1963.

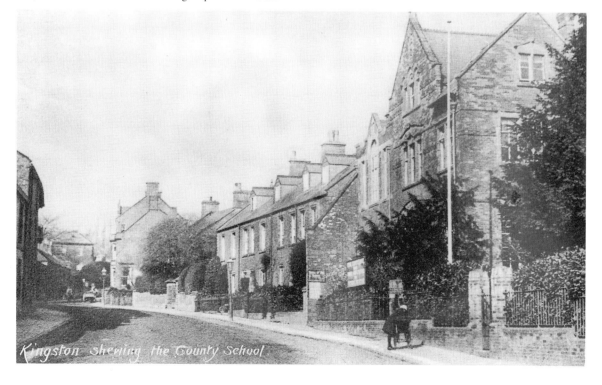

86. Reckleford School staff, September 1880. Reckleford School was built by Yeovil School Board, opening in 1874. It still stands opposite the fire and ambulance stations, though it is no longer a school. Mr. and Mrs. Higham, shown in this photograph, had been appointed on 14 October 1875, at a salary of '£170 for the first year, not including gas and coal'.

87. South Street Schools. A photograph by Henry Stiby, *c*.1880, of the Church of England establishment built as an infant and Sunday school in 1860, to cater for children living in Holy Trinity (Hendford) parish. Standing opposite Union Street, the buildings were demolished in 1965.

88. Yeovil Adult School Band. The Men's Adult School met on Sunday mornings in Hendford parish room. The two secretaries seated front centre were A. S. Macmillan and S. Burt. In 1905 they gave Saturday night concerts in the town hall, when admission was twopence! That year, the season concluded on Easter Monday with the special engagement of 'humorous entertainer' Fred Odell of London.

89. Wyndham Museum, once the billiard room of 28 Kingston. A bronze panel, from the former Borough Museum in King George Street, records the gift of the above by William Wyndham, Esq. to be the town's first museum. This was sold to assist in founding the later establishment.

90. An interior view of the original Wyndham Museum when it was in the billiard room of 28 Kingston. Among the exhibits displayed in the photograph are several which can be distinguished as being in the collection held by the Museum of South Somerset.

91. A view of the museum situated above the former Borough Public Library in King George Street. Mr. William Wyndham donated £2,000 from the sale of the Kingston property towards the setting up of the new museum. This, in turn, was transferred, in 1965, to what had been the coach-house of Hendford Manor—the present Museum of South Somerset.

Industry

Tanning and glove-making were certainly carried on here from at least the 14th century. Among those who rioted and attacked the bishop of the diocese and his entourage in 1349 for no apparent reason (though it may have been connected with the Statute of Labourers, following the Black Death), were Thomas and Nicholas Skynnare, Adam Tannere, Robert Bras, tanner, Hugh le Glovere and Philip Glovere. It is likely, though, that these products were for local use only. There is evidence to suggest that these trades were expanding in the 17th century and, by the 18th, had become 'a great trade'. Glove-making was to remain the town's staple industry until the beginning of the 20th century, and continued to thrive for a further 40 years, after which gradual decline finally resulted in the closure of Yeovil's last glove factory in 1989.

The growth of trade in the 19th century was fostered by the establishment of local banks, the earliest being Daniell & Hopkins' which became known as Yeovil Old Bank. This was followed shortly afterwards by Whitmash & White's Bank in 1808. Both these banks were taken over by Stuckey's Banking Company whose premises occupied the site of the *Angel Inn*, now the National Westminster. The Wilts & Dorset Bank opened in High Street in 1836 and, after other moves, finally occupied newly-built premises in The Borough in 1856—this became a branch of Lloyds Bank in 1914. The Capital & Counties Bank opened in 1897 in imposing premises on the corner of Princes and High Streets, which still retain the bank's emblem at the top of the building, though now occupied by the Bristol and West Building Society.

Local weekly newspapers also played an important part in promoting the town's trade and industry. A paper started in Yeovil as early as 1744 as *The Western Flying Post*, or *Yeovil Mercury* then moved to Sherborne only four and half years later; it was not until 1847, that another journal, *The Yeovil Times* was established. This paper acquired *The Western Flying Post* in 1851, and the two were amalgamated with offices in Princes Street. *The Western Gazette* came into being, in opposition, in 1863 and bought up *The Flying Post* four years later. Other papers which had some success before more modern 'freebies' included *The Western Chronicle* (1886-1931), *The Yeovil Leader* (1899-1924) and T*he Three Shires Advertiser* (1904-24).

The industry which took over from glove-making started, modestly enough, with James B. Petter being installed in an ironmonger's business in the borough. Extending its scope by manufacturing agricultural implements and machinery, the firm's foundry won nationwide recognition with the invention and production of the 'Nautilus' fire grate. Further inventions followed, notably a one-horse-power engine installed in a horseless carriage—one of the earliest in the country—and the production and development of a great number of very efficient stationary oil engines. So were laid the foundations of what became an aircraft company during the First World War, leading to that renowned organisation which is today's Westland Helicopters.

Another firm gaining countrywide fame was established in 1888 as the Western Counties Creameries, the proprietors, Messrs. Aplin & Barrett, at first marketing just cheese and butter, then adding other products, including the popular 'St Ivel' brand which from the start was a great success.

92. Photographed following the cessation of hostilities of the First World War, the woodworkers' department of Westland Aircraft thoughtfully included the date—21 November 1918—an all too rare occurrence in records of this nature.

93. Taken a week later than the above, members of the woodmill department of Westland Aircraft appear to be posed
in front of the identical aircraft.

94. Unlike the two preceding photographs, the propeller department of Westland Aircraft Works did not include the date, but it appears to have formed part of the same series, commissioned, no doubt, to record the workforce which in a short period had adapted itself to the successful production of aircraft to support the First World War effort.

95. Continuing with aircraft production, this Westland Widgeon, Mark IIIA, 1929, was the latest of the Widgeon monoplanes to be built by Westland Aircraft Company. This version was fitted with a Hermes engine.

96. Interceptor prototypes were built by the company in an endeavour to meet demands by the Royal Air Force for a fast-climbing high-altitude day fighter. This example, photographed on 22 June 1931, was powered by a Jupiter engine fitted with a Townsend ring.

97. The leather-dressing yard of Messrs. Blake & Fox's glove factory in Summerhouse Terrace in 1924. Here workers are attending to soaking and lime pits.

98. Messrs. Blake & Fox's unhairing department of their Summerhouse Terrace glove manufactory in 1924. Here skins were scraped free from hair and flesh prior to stretching; an unpalatable occupation accompanied by an evil-smelling atmosphere.

99. The wheeling department of Messrs. Blake & Fox's factory, where leather was given a final treatment before being passed on to the glove-cutters.

100. Glove-cutters at Messrs. Clothier & Giles glove factory, Addlewell Lane, in 1955. The high degree of skill required for this occupation is reflected in the weekly wages being paid in 1852, where cutters are placed at the top of the scale, receiving between 16s. and £1 2s., as compared with leather parers who could earn between 14s. and £1 a week.

101. Employees in the Eastland Road leather-dressing factory, built in 1850 for William Bide. The skill of a leather-dresser could earn him 14s. a week in 1826, as compared with a 'jobber', or labourer, who was only paid between 6s. and 8s.

102. *(Right)* Offices of Messrs. Brutton, Mitchell Tom Ltd., Princes Street, 1960. The brewery at the rear originated in the 19th century as Kitson and Cave's, subsequently Cave's, then Cave & Brutton, and J. Brutton & Son Ltd. before amalgamating. Finally, they were acquired by Charrington & Co. (South-West) Ltd. The lower portion of these buildings are now shop fronts.

103. *(Below)* This aerial perspective of Aplin & Barrett's Newton Road factory was drawn for them by S. Loxton in 1898. Its most famous product, St Ivel cheese, was first manufactured here, and the inclusion of a train, on the right, emphasised the proximity of the railway and prompt despatch of products to all parts of the country.

104. *(Below right)* The cheese-making department of Messrs. Aplin & Barrett's Western Counties Creameries, in Newton Road. It was in 1901 that the St Ivel brand name was first adopted. The name, based on an early version of the spelling of Yeovil, is not, however, to be found in any list of saints!

Bird's-eye View of Yeovil Premises

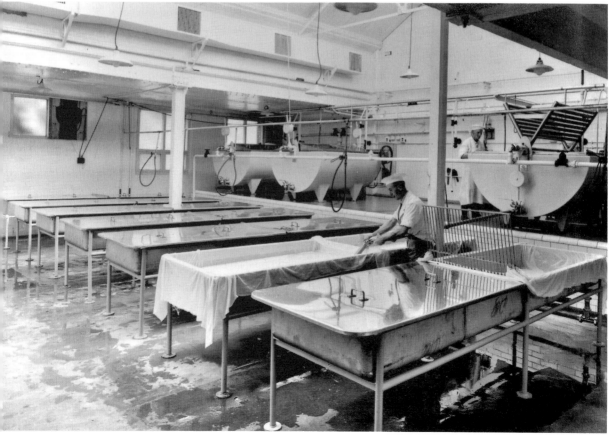

Before Supermarkets

Many of Yeovil's traders were prominent in the town's affairs. The Damon brothers, Robert and Edmund, for instance, were both members of the Volunteer Fire Brigade, having joined in April 1871. Robert became Brigade Lieutenant in 1875 and, ten years later, Captain. On his death in 1905, his brother, Edmund, took over that position, also serving as Mayor of Yeovil for three terms, in 1909, 1910 and 1916.

The Damons, like many of their contemporaries in outfitting and dressmaking, maintained a staff of workpeople engaged in bespoke tailoring. Thomas Thorne, who occupied premises on the corner of Middle and Silver Streets in 1890 (illustration 120), employed 'a large staff of experienced milliners and dressmakers, besides a gentlemen's outfitting department', where cutters and tailors, sitting cross-legged on a table, would be found sewing garments both by hand as well as by machine.

Indeed, during the 19th century, many shops employed craftsmen manufacturing goods on their premises, frequently to customers' specifications. Boots and shoes, pots, pans, baskets, hats and stays, as well as umbrellas and clocks were all locally produced, though in the case of clocks, mechanisms were generally bought and assembled, then mounted in town-made cases.

The temporary storage of customers' joints of meat in their cold store was one of the services offered by Hinton Farm Meat Supplies, Princes Street, in 1889, and 'Crystal Ice from Bath City Water, specially filtered for domestic use' was 'always for sale'.

Besides larger establishments, there were many individuals, frequently with assistance from their families, who lived over their shops, such as the Card family of tailors (illustration 106), as well, in the early days, as the Denners, drapers and outfitters. In developing suburbs, a front room was set aside by enterprising householders, like the Honeycombes in West Hendford (illustration 105), ready to supply the immediate needs of the neighbourhood.

Other traders, blessed with foresight, were ready to adapt to changing tastes or to invest in new developments, and to extend their range of goods as, for instance, Ince Gamis (illustration 113). Hardware merchants and smiths stocked sewing machines or bicycles, readily catering for a growing trade in 'motor spirit', like Moffatt's in High Street, Hyde & Wakely, the Triangle, and 'Herbie' Higdon, Middle Street. Music stores started to stock phonographs, then radios and, later still, television sets, and washing 'dollies' were replaced by ever more sophisticated washing machines. Multiple stores, like Maypole and International, gradually replaced local tradesmen and, in turn, were superseded by superstores.

The small-town trader, standing behind his counter, greeted most of his customers by name, and was ever ready to oblige; chairs were provided while parcels were wrapped in brown paper and tied with string—small ones finished with a loop to assist carrying—while more bulky purchases could almost always be delivered.

In larger shops, while this was being done, the bill (in pounds, shillings and pence) had been totted up, checked by an overseer, and taken, or placed in a cup and catapulted by means of overhead wires, to the cashier's desk, a receipt prepared and, with any change, returned by the same means. Drapers, whose bills frequently concluded with 11¾d., rounded up the sum by including a packet of pins in lieu of the farthing change.

105. Honeycombe's grocery store, West Hendford, *c*.1900, typical of many corner stores catering for the immediate needs of local residents. The lady in the doorway is Mrs. Bowden, whose daughter married the proprietor of the store.

106.   With a decidedly unbalanced appearance, apparently due to the erection of a two-storey extension to an older single-storey cottage, this tailor's business was situated between Hendford Terrace and the *Volunteer Tavern*. The Card family were well-known Yeovil tailors, with an additional shop in Middle Street, when this photograph was taken, *c*.1900.

07. Though both shops bear the joint initials of Robert and Edmund Damon, in High Street, they operated as separate
establishments. Robert at no.17, a silk mercer and costumier, etc., also attended to funerals ('Washington Funeral
'ar, Shillibeer and Mourning Coaches kept'), and Edmund at no.16 was a 'clerical and merchant tailor, hosier, and
'utfitter, etc.'

108. In 1903 Hubert John Moffatt was a cycle agent, and James Moffatt had a sewing-machine depot, both at no.4 High Street. Four years later, James was advertising sewing machines, cycles, mail carts, laundry appliances, motor sundries, and the supply of petrol. Later still a petrol pump was installed. These premises closed in 1972.

109. Work in progress in February 1934 to strengthen Messrs. Denners' stores in Hendford by the insertion of this immense steel girder. Since then, the whole of these Hendford premises have been incorporated in the store, including the shop occupied by Messrs. Parson & Shute, outfitters, who were followed by T. B. Lock, seedsman and florist.

110. Middle Street butcher, D. Lawrence, in 1935, when this picture was taken, reserved the window on the far side for the display of English meat, while the other was for showing 'Colonial Meat Only'. These premises exhibited a once-common type of building, with first-floor three-light windows, and graded stone tiles to the roof. Note the bar for meat-hanging.

111. Many tradesmen, where appropriate, augmented sales from their premises by providing the welcome service of carrying a display of wares to potential customers' doors. Here, Harold Robins is seen with such a handcart outside J. S. Robins' fish and fruit shop at no.1 Frederick Place.

112.   Corner stores, Sherborne Road, since demolished, was where T. W. Clements opened his grocery and provisions business in 1863. With another branch in High Street, he specialised in blends of tea, but lived up to the description of being 'supply stores' by also stocking hams, cheese, patent medicines, perfumes, brushes, enamels, and almost all other household goods.

113.   A congested High Street, c.1965, showing Gliddon's, Moffatt's, and Gamis's stores. The latter, by then house furnishers, originated with Ince Gamis, who is shown as a 'Perfumer, Hairdresser, and Toy Dealer' in 1830; later as just 'Toy Dealer', then 'Stationer and Toy Dealer', first at no.76 Hendford, next to the bank, and then, by 1914, at the High Street address.

114. Situated in the former Vicarage Street, now below the level of the Quedam Centre, these premises of Percy Winsor Ltd., agricultural implement agents and manufacturers, were enlarged by the acquisition of the one-time Unitarian chapel, seen here at the right of the show-rooms.

115. Boots the Chemists in the former 'Medical Hall', in The Borough; the premises extended into Wine Street. Note the circle in the foreground, a position reserved for point-duty policemen. These premises were destroyed by one of three bombs dropped in the area during an early morning raid on 12 April 1941.

116.   The south side of Middle Street, above Union Street, in 1932. The roadway was considerably narrower than now, and the photograph shows the International Stores being rebuilt. The former post office, now W. H. Smith & Son's premises, is totally obscured by the projection of the properties shown. On the far corner of Union Street is Gaylard's gentlemen's outfitters.

117.   The Yeovil and District Co-operative Society was first registered on 22 June 1889, and rented a shop in Middle Street on the site now occupied by Woolworth's. After a shaky start, the business expanded and in 1897 the first branch was opened in Orchard Street; the archway shown in the photograph led to a bakery and stables at the rear.

118.   In 1899 part of the buildings in the Triangle was acquired by the Co-operative Society, which was extended in 1910 to occupy the whole of the site. The photograph shows staff at the central premises in 1905 before the remainder of the building had been acquired. Various branches opened in other parts of the town, until consolidation in the present store adjoining Glovers' Walk.

119. Hinton Farm Meat Supply premises, Princes Street, with the Christmas display of meat and poultry in 1910. The then proprietor, J. H. Burrows, had succeeded George D. Dampney, who in 1880 advertised that, in summer months, 'pure Wenham lake ice' could always be obtained, and joints hung in his ice-house for customers' convenience.

120. Top of Middle Street, c.1890. Standing on the left, 'London House' was occupied by Thomas Thorne, draper, milliner, dress and mantle maker, and gents' outfitter. He had followed George and Robert Wadman, who claimed to have been established in 1645, and Thorne's successors were Hartree & Son. On the opposite corner, Gatward & Wright, chemists, stand next to the International Stores.

121. Lower Middle Street looking towards the Triangle, c.1965. Shortly afterwards (1967-8) the whole of this side of the street was redeveloped and the area has since become a pedestrian precinct. Few of the traders then occupying these premises survived the change for long.

122. Lower Middle Street looking in the opposite direction to the preceding illustration, and taken at the same time. These premises, too, were included in the redevelopment, none of the small traders shown survives today. The Co-operative Stores, on the left, almost immediately vacated those premises.

123. Lower Middle Street, *c*.1965. The two blocks between Soyers and the Liberal Club were demolished for the building of Tesco Stores, which has since moved to a more extensive location. Builders' merchants A. D. May Ltd. occupied the former monumental works of Appleby & Childs, and the large building beyond once housed the offices and printing works of the *Western Chronicle* group of newspapers.

Spiritual Needs

Though a Saxon church is known to have existed in Yeovil in A.D. 950, the present church of St John the Baptist dates from the end of the 14th century. Yeovil's oldest building, in early Perpendicular style, with many large windows, earned for itself the title of 'Lantern of the West'.

New parishes, embracing growing suburbs, led to the building of Holy Trinity church for Hendford in 1846, and St Michael and All Angels, Pen Mill, in 1897.

The short-lived Reformed Episcopalian Christ Church, in The Park, lasted for just 25 years, while the Roman Catholic community, returning to Yeovil after 300 years as a mission in 1887, rented The Chantry for services, continuing there for seven years until the Church of the Holy Ghost was opened in 1899.

Nonconformity flourished in the 17th century, Baptists were holding meetings in Yeovil in 1656, and a South Street barn was used as a meeting place from 1668 until it was replaced by a chapel in 1717. Quakers regularly met in various houses at about the same time, a burial ground being obtained in 1669, and a meeting-house established in Kingston by *c*.1700.

Following the Restoration in 1662, congregations broke away from the parish church and established a Unitarian chapel in Vicarage Street; a Congregational chapel in Clarence Street followed in 1793, and a Calvinist chapel in Tabernacle Lane in 1804.

The first Methodist meeting-house was built on a bank above Middle Street in 1824, being replaced by the present Vicarage Street church, which opened in 1870. 'Daughter' churches and meeting places of other denominations have been installed in several parts of the town, where they continue to flourish.

124. St John the Baptist parish church, before 1856. Noticeable differences between then and now are the absence of headstones, the chantry chapel and, between it and the south porch, a tiny fire-engine house. The south porch, rebuilt in 1861, was then surmounted by a sundial, while the former Silver Street entrance to the churchyard can be seen extreme right.

125. Yeovil's expanding 19th-century population and St John's overflowing congregation led to the building of a new church. The foundation stone of Holy Trinity was laid on 24 June 1843 and, following the formal creation of Hendford as a separate parish on 22 September 1846, the completed church was consecrated on 28 October.

126. Holy Trinity church interior, *c*.1880. Designed by Benjamin Ferrey in the Early English style, this interior view shows the bench seating then installed and the chancel before it was enclosed in 1896 by a wrought-iron screen, extended in 1906. Visible, too, is the earlier reredos which was replaced in 1897 by fine carved oak with painted panels.

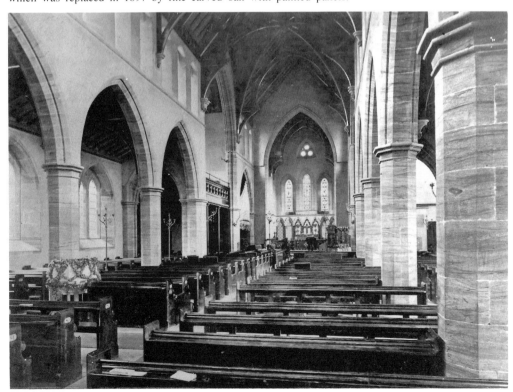

127.   A Henry Stiby photograph of Christ Church (Reformed Episcopal) and adjoining properties in The Park, soon after their erection in 1880. Demolished in 1905, the fabric of the church was utilised in the building of Christchurch Villas, which in turn were taken down for the construction of Queensway.

128.   Possibly the only surviving picture of the interior of Christ Church, also taken by Henry Stiby, soon after its construction. This faded print shows the nave and chancel with its polygonal apse. This church, too, was designed in the Early English style and built of Hamstone. The building costs of the church and adjoining schools, are said to have been about £3,600.

129. Vicarage Street Unitarian chapel, erected in 1809 on property purchased for the congregation in 1704. Substantially altered in 1893, it was later sold and for some years used as an extension of Percy Winsor's agricultural machinery depot before being demolished for the construction of the Quedam Centre. During excavations for the latter in 1983, a burial, believed to be that of Robert Batten, was uncovered.

130. The buildings, centre right, in this 1965 photograph of Clarence Street include the first Congregational (now United Reformed) church in Yeovil, built in 1793 and entered through the pedimented archway. The present church, built at the rear of this building with an entrance from Princes Street, superseded it in 1878. The buildings shown here were demolished in 1979.

131. Yeovil's first Methodist meeting-house still remained hemmed in by later buildings, even when the present Methodist church was opened in Vicarage Street in March 1870. It is here seen standing above the furniture and bedding department of the Co-operative Society (earlier Jesty's) where it remained until these buildings were pulled down in 1980 and replaced by a modern building.

132. Sunday School scholars photographed outside the Pen Mill Methodist chapel in Lyde Road; the date appears to be just before the First World War. The chapel was demolished in 1983. A newspaper of 13 January 1889 reported the opening of a 'new Wesleyan Mission Chapel in London Road opposite Great Western Terrace'.

133. Henry Stiby is here seen performing the official opening of the new Salvation Army Hall at the junction of Sherborne Road and Southville in 1932. He is accompanied by Alderman W. E. Tucker. Prior to this the Salvation Army had occupied former *Western Gazette* premises on the corner of Newton Road and Middle Street.

Health and Welfare

The prevalance of plague in the 16th century is shown by several references in Yeovil's churchwardens' accounts. In 1578, when there was a surplus over expenditure of £17 0s. 8d., there is a note at the end:

> Memorandum at the End of this Acct. by the consent of the whole Pshe, there was paide out of the foresaid sum of £17 0s. 8d. towards the relief and sustentation of divers poor people visited by the plage this yere and for the buylding a House for them uppon Doddam, the sum of £11 0s. 9d.

Dodham was then quite remote and separated from the town (as now) by a brook. This is the first recorded instance in Yeovil of a building specially erected to isolate sufferers from the plague; generally they were shut up in their own homes until they recovered or died!

Prone to epidemics from medieval days, Yeovil's working population was just as susceptible even in the middle of the 19th century. Rapid expansion within the confined space of the borough had not been answered by the provision of better living conditions. The Rammell report of 1852 revealed a high incidence of tuberculosis and outbreaks of cholera and typhoid, largely the result of overcrowding and lack of proper sewerage and sanitation.

After Yeovil became a municipal corporation in 1854, boundaries were extended and healthier conditions were created by improvements in sewerage and a supply of pure water.

A dispensary for out-patients opened in a Kingston cottage in 1858, followed by the provision in 1872 of Yeovil's first hospital at Fiveways. Acquisition of Kingston Manor House and grounds allowed for a more extensive general hospital, which was opened by the Prince of Wales in 1923. Though extended from time to time, half a century later it proved inadequate to meet modern demands, and the present hospital replaced it in 1973.

Compassion for the elderly and poor led charitably-minded clergy to establish two almshouses in the 15th century. The earlier, long known as the Portreeve's almshouse, was founded by John Stone, rector of Tintinhull *c.*1416. Formerly in South Street, it was replaced in 1910 by a more commodious building of six self-contained flats in Preston Grove.

The other foundation, dating from 1477, was by John Woborn and Richard Huett, chaplains, in memory of Canon William Woborn. Originally sited at the foot of Silver Street, it was moved to Bond Street in 1860.

Yeovil's first known workhouse was established early in the 19th century in Vicarage Street, close to the present Methodist church. It was later replaced by a building off lower Middle Street—a site at the rear of the present Liberal Club—this too became redundant after the opening of Yeovil Union Workhouse in Preston Road in 1837. An advertisement of 1844 for a schoolmaster for this establishment stated that applicants for the post were required to teach the three R's and tailoring to the pauper children. The salary was to be £20 per annum plus board.

Yeovil Day Centre, originally a temperance hall, is also available for the use of today's elderly people.

34. Fiveways hospital, photographed by Henry Stiby, *c.*1880. Opened in 1872, it remained Yeovil's hospital until
1922 when a new building opened in Kingston Manor grounds. The Fiveways hospital then continued as a maternity
ome until the present unit opened in 1968. Demolished in 1969, the site of the old building was lost in constructing
he Fiveways roundabout.

135. H.R.H. the Prince of Wales, later Edward VIII, opening the doors of Yeovil General Hospital on 19 July 1923. Though Kingston Manor House and grounds had been acquired in 1916, construction of the new hospital was delayed because of the war, and the foundation stone was not laid until 1921.

136. Photographed in 1965, this shows the Higher Kingston entrance to the former Yeovil General Hospital. Already the site in the foreground was being cleared in preparation for the construction of the boiler-house for the new district hospital. Stonework seen here, above the archway, was preserved and built into the entrance to the present hospital car park.

137. Woborn Almshouse, Bond Street. The original 1477 foundation, at the junction of Silver Street and Market Street, at the rear of the *Pall Tavern* was replaced by this more commodious building in 1860, the medieval premises having become dilapidated. They had provided accommodation for 'twelve poor people of both sexes, equal in number, single and chaste, and untainted by leprosy'.

138. A modernisation programme for Woborn Almshouse, in the 1970s, provided eight self-contained flats for both single and married persons chosen, as originally, from 'poor persons of good character who had resided in the ancient parish of Yeovil for at least five years'. This photograph shows the newly-renovated common room before its final decoration.

139. Henry Stiby, with trowel in hand, had just laid the foundation stone of Dorcas House in Preston Grove on 27 July 1910. Providing six self-contained flats, this replaced the former Portreeve's (Corporation) Almshouses, South Street, which, as it happened, was burnt down that same year. It is now certain they had been founded, 1416, by John Stone, rector of Tintinhull.

140. The foundation stone of Union Street Victoria Temperance Hall was laid by Lady Theodora Guest in 1887 and opened in 1889 as headquarters of the local temperance society and Band of Hope. It was also used, at the beginning of the century, for day and evening classes of the 'Government Art and Science School', and is now Yeovil Day Centre.

Matters Martial

In the middle ages able-bodied and trained men were required to form part of the national militia. There are no accounts, however, of any locally-raised troops engaged in battle until comparatively recent times.

Yeovil men may well have taken part in the Civil Wars, and certainly a number were with Monmouth's troops at the Battle of Sedgemoor.

At the time of the Napoleonic wars the threat of invasion led to the formation of a volunteer defence organisation and, in 1794, Yeovil raised a troop of Gentlemen and Yeomanry Cavalry. When invasion was believed to be imminent in 1803, there was an enthusiastic response, resulting in some 20,000 enrolments in Somerset volunteer units. In that year, the Yeovil sub-division of the Regiment of Volunteer Infantry consisted of eight companies each of 60 privates. Under the command of local gentlemen officers, they were kept in a constant state of readiness.

Wagons were requisitioned from local owners and fitted with plank seats, supplied by the government, to provide transport for troops or to evacuate civilians. However, when the threat did not materialise, troops attended a thanksgiving service, and the regiment was disbanded in 1808.

In 1859 several corps of rifle volunteers were being formed in the county, among them the 16th (Yeovil) R.V.C. under the captaincy of Thomas Messiter, of Barwick, Lieutenant Donne and Ensign White. Bands formed by members or units of this volunteer corps attended popular functions, while rifle contests were also held between 'regulars' and 'honorary' members.

A squadron of West Somerset Yeomanry had its headquarters in Yeovil in 1908, and objected strongly to Dorset Yeomanry recruiting in Yeovil, but, despite a Commons statement that recruiting should be confined to the respective counties, Dorset Yeomanry continued to maintain a drill station in Yeovil. Of two Territorial battalions of eight companies each formed at this time, Yeovil Company was part of the 5th Battalion of Prince Albert's Somerset Light Infantry.

At the outbreak of the First World War there was again great patriotic fervour and a ready response to recruiting campaigns. National Reservists received their colours, and 'Kitchener's recruits' marched through the streets, with a band playing, on their way to entrain at Yeovil Town station. Horses were selected for cavalry and draught purposes. Almost at once, the resources of the Petter organisation were placed at the government's disposal, munitions were manufactured at the Reckleford Nautilus works, and the new Westland factory was devoted to aircraft production.

The British Red Cross Society set up a fully-equipped hospital, with 62 beds, in the Newnam Memorial Hall in January 1915 where 1,200 casualties from the front received treatment. Closed in December 1918, it was staffed throughout the war by members of the Somerset V.A.D. units, and the building was provided free of charge by the Baptist church.

The Second World War saw two training camps established nearby at Houndstone and Lufton. The town itself sustained ten air raids resulting in 49 deaths, 122 injuries and 2,754 damaged houses, including 68 which were totally destroyed—in all a third of the borough's houses.

After the end of the war in Europe, celebrations were held on 8 May 1945, when a huge crowd gathered in The Borough to hear an address by the Mayor, Alderman W. S. Vosper. Later, there was dancing in the former market square. In addition to street parties for children, there was a civic welcome home for those returning from the services, each receiving a leather wallet or note-case bearing the town crest.

141. Yeovil Military Band in the grounds of Hendford Manor, 1892. This photograph was taken by C. J. Trask, who was then Lieutenant (he later became Captain) of F Company, 2nd Battalion P.A.S.L.I. The armoury in The Park by this time had been given up for premises in South Street.

142.   Generally known as Yeovil's Military Band, photographed some time prior to the outbreak of the First World War, its official designation was the band of Yeovil F Company Volunteers of Prince Albert's Somerset Light Infantry. The Bandmaster's name was Beare.

143. National Reservists assembled in The Borough on Bank Holiday Monday, 4 August 1914, before proceeding to Taunton to receive their colours. War against Germany was declared at midnight.

144. 'Kitchener's Army' recruits, awaiting the arrival of a train at Yeovil Town station in 1914 to carry them to a training centre. They were watched by a group standing on the roof of a carriage in the siding, which bears a notice proclaiming, 'Well done Yeovil, we are proud of you'.

"THE WAR" GOVERNMENT INSPECTOR SELECTING HORSES at YEOVIL, AUG 5TH 1914

145. Britain declared war on Germany on 4 August 1914 and, as an inscription on the photograph shows, a government inspector was at Yeovil the following day selecting horses for the use of the army.

146. Following the outbreak of the First World War, the entire resources of the Petter organisation were placed at the disposal of the government, both at the Nautilus works, Reckleford, and the newly-erected Westland factory. This photograph shows shell cases being produced at the Nautilus works.

147. Officers and members of Yeovil V.A.D. Som/80 (Women's) and Som/19 (Men's) sections who staffed the British Red Cross Society's auxiliary hospital which was established, free of charge, in the Newnam Memorial Hall adjoining South Street Baptist church, from 1915 to 1918.

148.   Following several 'alerts' of impending raids during the Second World War, and the Royal
Observer Corps' assurance to foreman Stone that a warning of imminent danger would be given to
Rickett's glove factory, Addlewell Lane, the foreman and girls emerged to watch a 'dog fight' over the
town, during which a bomb, which did not explode, fell on the building they had vacated.

149.   Another 1940 photograph by Harry Stone, of bomb damage to Rickett's glove factory in Addlewell
Lane. Two bombs had been dropped in the area, one in the factory's leather-dressing yard, and the other
behind houses in Park Street. Neither bomb exploded.

150. With the odd name of Picketty Row, in Wellington Street, these houses, with air-raid shelters in front of them, were demolished in 1955. Although the majority of similar shelters have suffered the same fate, there are still several surviving in gardens at the present time.

151. A fortnight's drive for unwanted books, held in 1943, resulted in 75,000 being received at the Newnam Hall depot. Of these 7,000 were recovered for despatch to the Armed Forces, a further 1,500 being reserved to help restock bombed libraries. The remainder, rejected by a 'scrutiny committee' under librarian, A. E. Batty, were recycled to aid the war effort.

152.   Yeovil Borough Company Home Guard, Q Section, No.5 Platoon pictured in December 1944. Founded in May 1940 as Local Defence Volunteers, the latter name was adopted three months later. This company was disbanded a year after the group shown here was photographed.

153.   Yeovil Borough Fire Guard outside their South Street office in May 1945. Fire-watching was made compulsory on 31 December 1940, and posts were established on the roofs of many Yeovil buildings. Watch continued to be maintained until the end of the war, though the town's last air raid occurred on 5 August 1942, when nearly 1,000 houses were damaged.

154. The Mayor, Alderman W. S. Vosper, giving an address to the huge crowd assembled in The Borough to celebrate V.E. day on 8 May 1945. Children are shown in pride of place at the front of staging erected on the bombed site at the corner of Middle Street and The Borough.

155. As part of the V.E. day celebrations, a civic service was held on Yeovil Town football ground in Huish, when various organisations attended. Here, members of the Home Guard and other voluntary services are seen proceeding from Westminster Street to take part.

56.   Following addresses by civic leaders at the Victory-in-Europe celebrations, dancing took place in the centre of the
rowded Borough, as shown in this photograph. Providing a dramatic back-drop is the site of the bomb-destroyed premises
f the former 'Medical Hall' of Boots the Chemists. For a few years following, this was laid out as a flower bed.

157.   V.E. celebrations—music for dancing, which was taking place just around the corner, was provided by this dance band at the top of Middle Street. At the back, youngsters have climbed on to a sign advertising lunches at the British Restaurant.

158.   Street parties to mark the victorious end of the war were held in many of Yeovil's residential areas. The crowd assembled here attended such a gathering, which was held in the garden of Mr. and Mrs. R. W. Sweet's home at 37 Orchard Street.

Red-Letter Days

Among regular events which were looked forward to with great anticipation were the annual share-outs of friendly societies and the convivial celebrations which accompanied them. In 1892, an old Yeovilian, remembering vanished features of his youth, spoke of two such societies, 'the old *Mermaid* club, or Yeovil Guardian Friendly Society, and the *Pall* club, or Yeovil True Blue Friendly Society'. Their members paraded the streets carrying club brasses and banners with a band playing, the former on Whit-Monday and the latter on the following day. On both occasions 'hundreds of people from far and near' came into town to witness the events.

Such events in the life of the town, passed on by word of mouth to children and grandchildren, were also recorded in the local press. Well written and detailed accounts appeared in print, though such reports were not illustrated by photographs until the early years of the present century. It was left to professional photographers to record eventful scenes, who then sold their prints to those wishing to preserve a visual record.

When the local press started to include photographs, they were often supplied by national agencies, such as on the occasion of the accession of King Edward VII in 1901. By the time of King George V's succession in 1910, and of his coronation the following year, although the *Western Gazette* had established its own photographic block-making department, it still relied on agency material, and no local pictures appeared; so, once more, it was the local photographer who recorded scenes in the borough and elsewhere.

On the occasion of a coronation, which followed about a year after the accession of a new sovereign—in order to allow a period of mourning for the predecessor—the town's thoroughfares and many individual houses were bedecked with bunting, 'triumphal arches' spanned many streets, each area endeavouring to exceed the splendour of their neighbours, and prizes were awarded for the most attractive. Such occasions were marked with teas for children and poor folk, who were presented with decorated mugs bearing portraits of the King and Queen; in addition special commemorative medals were struck, attached to ribbons. Carnival-like processions paraded through the town, and on at least one occasion the local weekly paper mounted a printing press on a float to produce a 'miniature edition' for distribution as it passed along. Such a day usually concluded with a firework display and a bonfire on Summerhouse Hill.

An important event of a political nature was recorded by an 'outsider' photographer. This shows the start of a procession in Newton Road on 'Labour Sunday' 1914, attended by a large number of local trade union members. A mass meeting, held in Huish, was addressed by several national trade union leaders in support of the current strike in London.

The local paper did not print photographs during the First World War, due to a shortage of materials, and only resumed after the Second World War. So, again, it was left to others to record events pictorially, such as the discovery of the Westland Roman site and other 'red-letter days' leading up to the accession of Queen Elizabeth II.

159.   Celebrating Queen Victoria's golden jubilee in Wyndham Fields in 1887, where tables and marquees provided teas and entertainment. In view of recent controversy over the granting of planning permission for the building of a superstore here, the inclusion of this photograph seems an important reminder of past gatherings, despite the somewhat poor quality of the original.

160.   The accession of a new monarch, since early times, has been an occasion of great importance, none more so than that of Edward VII—for such an event had not occurred in 64 years—since Queen Victoria was proclaimed in 1837. This large gathering of townspeople crowded The Borough to hear the announcement in January 1901.

161. Perhaps one should never be astonished at the vagaries of British weather since fluctuations have regularly—or rather, irregularly—occurred since records have been kept. Such an occasion is well-illustrated by this photograph of Hendford Manor House, taken on 25 April 1908, yet only a week later, on 1 May, the temperature was 75 degrees Fahrenheit in the shade!

162. Coronation day of King George V was marked on 22 July 1911 by a special gathering of schoolchildren in Preston Park. Early rain curtailed some of the planned events, though others were transferred under cover. The decoration of business premises and dwelling-houses was encouraged by prizes of between £5 and 10s. The day ended with a bonfire on Summerhouse Hill.

163. This undated photograph is believed to have been taken between 1908 and 1912, and shows a traditional annual Boxing Day Meet of the Blackmore Vale Hunt in The Borough. Large crowds always turned up for the event.

LABOR-DAY AT YEOVIL 1914

164. 'Labour Sunday', 3 May 1914. Procession in Newton Road, organised by South Somerset Trades and Labour Council, headed by Yeovil Town Band, setting off for the Corporation recreation ground, Huish, where a crowd of 1,200 included trade union members from Yeovil and neighbourhood. They were addressed by Charles Duncan M.P., of the Workers' Union, supported by several national trade union leaders.

165. In 1925, Yeovil Borough Council purchased land in Westland Road for housing development. The earlier discovery of a hoard of Roman coins there led Alderman W. R. E. Mitchelmore to carry out preliminary excavations which revealed extensive Roman foundations. Further excavations by Dr. Ralegh Radford, in 1927 and 1928 revealed a large Roman farmstead. Here, Alderman Mitchelmore is examining a pavement in room 23.

166. In days when Bath and West Agricultural Show visited different venues, Yeovil was twice host for its staging. On the first occasion, in 1856, it was held in Ram Park, and the second, in 1932 (Ram Park being no longer in existence), it was held in Barwick Park, the opening being performed by Mayor W. E. Tucker, shown here.

67. The ceremonial naming of a new 'County' class railway engine, *Yeovil*, took place at Yeovil Town station on
   November 1945. The Hon. Clive Pearson, director of the Southern Railway Company, attended by the Mayor,
V. S. Vosper, Town Clerk, Col. H. C. C. Batten, and members of the town council, is shown addressing an assembled
rowd, including schoolchildren.

168. The Mayor, Alderman Stanley H. Vincent, attended by the mayor's chaplain and members of the Corporation, at the proclamation of the accession of Queen Elizabeth II in February 1952.

169. Besides the town centre, many of Yeovil's residential areas decorated their streets for the coronation of the Queen on 2 June 1953. Among the most impressive was that of Wellington Street, shown here.

Social Occasions

In the 16th and 17th centuries, one of the main social events was undoubtedly the annual church sale of ale held on Ascension Day, when money was raised to assist the upkeep of the church. Churchwardens' accounts show some £10 (a large sum in the 16th century) being raised annually by this event, when a prominent townsman assumed the role of Robin Hood and, assisted by 'merry men', Maid Marian and a 'Prize Maid', led archery contests, produced a 'mystery play' and promoted the sale of ale brewed in the Parish House.

At other times the arrival of strolling players with a portable 'theatre' provided entertainment for several days at a time. That might have been such an occasion when certain 'strangers' paid 1s. 8d. in 1591 for a peal to be rung on the church bells 'when the Monster was in the Churchyard'. Itinerant actors continued to perform in a temporary theatre, set up in a yard on the site now occupied by Central Road, right up to the beginning of the present century.

The opening in High Street in 1849 of a Town Hall with a large assembly room, permitted balls and other entertainments to be staged. Bazaars in private grounds were a popular means of fund raising for various purposes—a two-day event of this kind was held in the extensive grounds of Braggchurch, the mayor's residence on Hendford Hill, in 1901.

Outdoor leisure activities were a much more important feature of everyday life before radio and television brought sport and entertainment into the home, whilst the train and motor car provided the opportunity to travel further afield than had been available previously to the majority.

During a hard winter, as in 1891-2, it cost nothing more than the hire of skates to gather on the thick ice of the frozen river Yeo to enjoy skating. Regular Saturday afternoon excursions, run by the licensee of a local hostelry, were forerunners of motor coach outings.

Group activities were catered for by a considerable number of organisations. Rifle Volunteers provided scope for marksmen to compete, a Thursday football club gave those who were free on early-closing days the opportunity to indulge in that sport. Saturday athletics were available for others to take part in running, as in the marathon held on 28 March 1914. Cycling enthusiasts had regular Sunday excursions and Mudford Road recreation ground opened in 1931 for appropriate seasonal activities.

In 1895 a football team played its first season at Pen Mill athletic ground as the Yeovil Casuals, changing its name to Yeovil Town Football Club in 1907. Rivalry developed with another club, which started in 1908 as Petter's United, and only ended when the two clubs were amalgamated in 1914 as Yeovil and Petters United. This title was retained until the end of the Second World War. Then, as Yeovil Town, the team achieved fame in the 1948-9 season as the 'giant-killers', reaching the fifth round of the F.A. Cup, when they played against cup-holders Manchester United, being beaten 8-0.

170. Periods of severely cold weather were experienced in the winters of 1890-1 and again in 1891-2. It was towards the end of 1891 that the river Yeo became so frozen as to support skaters and others, as shown here, on the thick ice at Cricketsham Bridge, which then carried the railway line between the Town station and Yeovil Junction.

171. The licensee of the *Red Lion Inn* is holding the reins ready to set out on a Saturday afternoon excursion in 1893. Mr. Brown owned a team of four horses and operated a twice-daily carrier service to Taunton, changing horses at Curry Rivel. He was reputed to have been the owner of the first commercial motor car in Yeovil.

72.   Marksmen of 1894 pose in mufti with their rifles to mark the occasion of a contest between 'regulars' of F
ompany, 2nd Battalion, Yeovil Rifle Volunteers, Somerset Light Infantry, and 'honorary' members of the same
ompany. The firing took place at Yeovil Marsh rifle range.

173. Yeovil Thursday Football Club, who were champions of the Taunton and District League in the 1912-13 season. Referee G. Rogers is on the extreme left back row, and Hon. Secretary, A. E. Dawe, is fifth from left. Chairman W. Pounds and treasurer C. E. Causer are first and second respectively front row, captain G. Priddle being third right.

74. The start of the marathon race from the top of High Street in 1914 seems to have attracted only four participants, though seen off by a crowd of supporters. The gentleman on the left, holding a handkerchief, seems to have been the starter, next to him in bowler hat an organiser, and next again a reporter with notebook in hand.

75. An opening match at the inauguration of Yeovil Bowling Club in 1909 on their green, then situated on grounds adjacent to the former recreation ground in Huish, remembered by many as Yeovil fairground—now part of Tesco's car park. The club moved to Higher Kingston in 1929-30, when activities were extended to include tennis.

176. *(Right)* Yeovil Cycling Club members photographed just before setting out on a Sunday morning in 1931. The meeting place was in lower Middle Street at the entrance to Station Road. The donor of the photograph, Dr. D. Chapman, is fourth from the left, holding a wheel—he had just mended a puncture!

177. *(Below)* The mayor, Alderman W. E. Tucker, opens 18 acres of land as Mudford Road Recreation Ground in June 1931. Since then it has become Yeovil Recreation, Athletics and Sports Centre of 40 acres, including a 400-metre all-weather athletic track with facilities for field events, in addition to soccer, rugby, cricket and hockey pitches, and tennis courts, golf facilities and a children's play area.

178. *(Below right)* Yeovil football fans arriving at Manchester for the fifth round proper of the F.A. Cup in the 1948-9 season. Watched by a crowd of 81,565, though they were defeated eight goals to nil by the cup-holders, Manchester United, the 'Glovers' were not disgraced, and in the same season won the Southern League Cup for the first time.

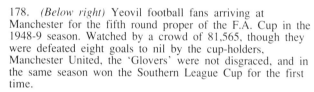

Select Bibliography

Brooke, L., *Somerset Newspapers 1725-1960* (1960)

Brooke, L. (ed.), *Yeovil: The Changing Scene* (1980)

Brooke, L., *Street Names in Yeovil* (1979)

Brooke, L., *Yesterday's Yeovil and its Traders* (1983)

Brooke, L., *Yesterday's Yeovil* (1989)

Clemas, F. M. (ed.), *Old Yeovil* (1987)

Day, J. H., *Steam Around Yeovil, the Final Days* (1985)

Evans, M. J., *Yeovil in Old Picture Postcards* (1992)

Gerard, T., *A Particular Description of Somerset* 1633 (Somerset Record Society XV, 1900)

Goodchild, J. *et al, The Borough of Yeovil* (1954)

Hayward, L. C., *Yeovil Almshouses* (1976)

Hayward, L. C., *From Portreeve to Mayor* (1987)

Hayward, L. C. and McDowell, R. W., *The George Hotel, Yeovil* (1962)

Heath, F. R., *Yeovil with its Surroundings* (1906)

James, D. N., *Westland Aircraft since 1915* (1991)

Kemble, R. G. (ed.), *Yeovil 1939-45* (1946)

Monday, D., *Planemakers 2—Westland* (1991)

Rammell, T. W., *Report into ... the Sanitary Conditions of the Inhabitants of the Parish of Yeovil* (1842)

Vickery, D., *A Sketch of the Town of Yeovil* (1856)

Warbis, A. T., *An Illustrated Guide to Yeovil and Neighbourhood* (1926)

Western Gazette files

Whitby & Son, *Almanacks* (1882-1919)

Drawn by T. Jerome

This somewhat romantic lithograph, drawn by T. Jerome, shows Yeovil from just over the Dorset border, with the Sherborne and London coach road leading out on the right. Dating from about 1830; tree-crowned Wyndham Hill is still untouched by the cutting of a railway track, and isolated Pen Mill lies at its foot.